RiverStream Science

DO YOU REALLY WANT TO MEET A PLATYPUS?

WRITTEN BY CARI MEISTER   ILLUSTRATED BY DANIELE FABBRI

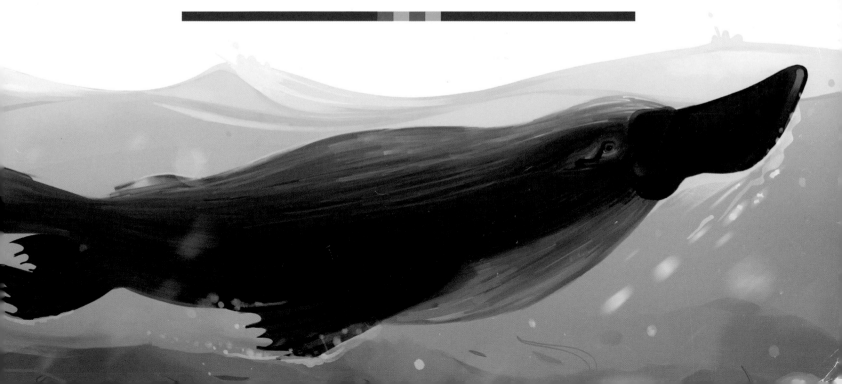

RiverStream Science
Great Reading • Real Learning

Amicus Illustrated hardcover edition is published by
Amicus. P.O. Box 1329, Mankato, MN 56002
www.amicuspublishing.us

RiverStream Publishing reprinted with permission of
Amicus Publishing.

Library of Congress Cataloging-in-Publication Data
Meister, Cari, author.
 Do you really want to meet a platypus? / by Cari
Meister ; illustrated by Daniele Fabbri.
    pages cm. — (Do you really want to meet?)
 Summary: "A child goes on an adventure to Austra-
lia in search of a duck-billed platypus, which is hard
to spot in the wild"— Provided by publisher.
 Audience: Grade K to 3.
 Includes bibliographical references and index.
 ISBN 978-1-60753-460-0 (library binding : alk.
paper) — ISBN 978-1-60753-675-8 (ebook)
1. Platypus—Juvenile literature. 2. Australia—Juvenile
literature. I. Fabbri, Daniele, illustrator. II. Title.
 QL737.M72M45 2015
 599.2'9—dc23   2013034704

Editor: Rebecca Glaser
Designer: Kathleen Petelinsek

1 2 3 4 5 CG 18 17 16 15 14
RiverStream Publishing–Corporate Graphics,
Mankato, MN—042014
ISBN 978-1-62243-229-5 (paperback)

ABOUT THE AUTHOR

Cari Meister is the author of more than 120 books for children, including the *Tiny* series and *My Pony Jack*. She lives in Evergreen, CO and Minnetrista, MN with her husband, John, their four sons, one dog, one horse, and 4 hamsters. You can visit her online at www.carimeister.com.

ABOUT THE ILLUSTRATOR

Daniele Fabbri was born in Ravenna, Italy, in 1978. He graduated from Istituto Europeo di Design in Milan, Italy, and started his career as a cartoon animator, storyboarder, and background designer for animated series. He has worked as a freelance illustrator since 2003, collaborating with international publishers and advertising agencies.

Have you ever heard of an animal with the bill of a duck, the tail of a beaver, and the body of an otter? No, it's not made up. It really does exist!

It's a **platypus**! Playtpuses are mammals, like dogs and people. They have hair and feed their young milk. But did you know that platypuses lay eggs like lizards do? They kind of walk like lizards, too.

What? You really want to meet a platypus?

EGGS

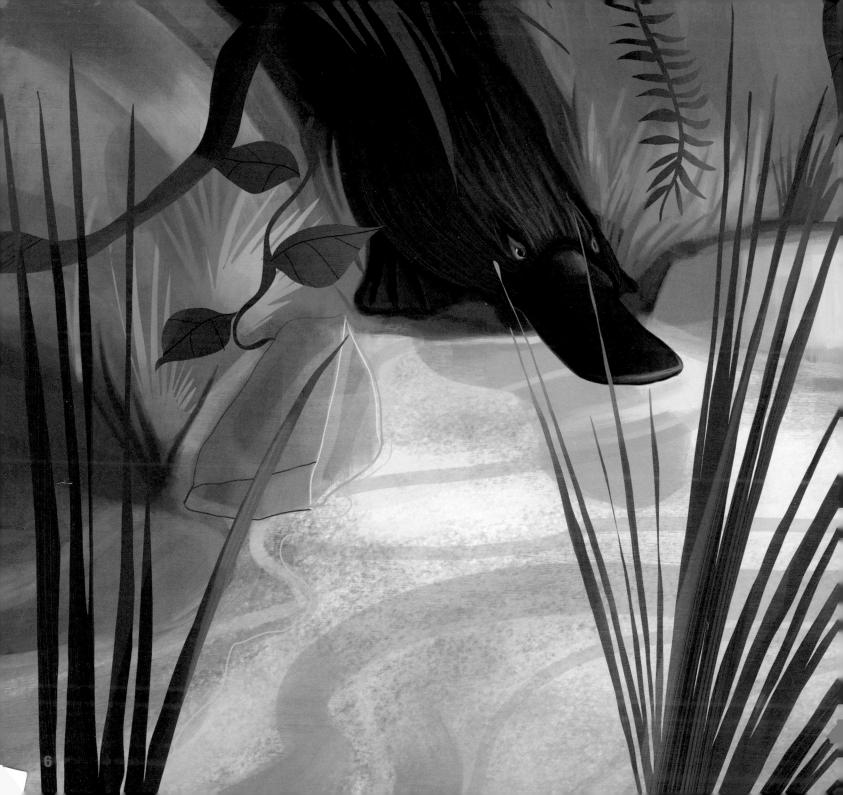

That might be tricky. Platypuses are *very* shy. If they see you coming, they will hide. Do you have night vision goggles? Platypuses are nocturnal—that means they are more active at night. And did I mention that platypuses ONLY live in Australia?

What? You've always wanted to go
"down under?" Right-o, mate! Gather
your things. You'll need waterproof shoes.

Platypuses live near lakes, streams, and rivers. They build their burrows next to the water. Get comfy. We're in for a long trip. It takes about 20 hours to fly to eastern Australia.

We made it! But I don't think we'll see any platypuses this time of day. They're sleeping cozily in their burrows now.

11

Let's look for tracks. Platypuses have webbed feet like ducks, but when they walk on land, they pull back the webbing and turn their toes under. Check out these prints. Are they platypus prints?

No, those tracks are too big.
They belong to that wombat over there.

These look like platypus tracks.
Let's follow them . . . but WAIT!

Did you know that male platypuses have venom? It's in the sharp pointy spikes on their ankles, and they can use it to poison their enemies. Don't worry, the venom won't kill you, but it can hurt very much. The venom *can* kill a fox or snake though.

Are you sure you STILL want to meet a platypus?

Well, now *would* be a good time to see one. Let's hide. That tangle of roots and mud over there looks like a platypus burrow.

If we're lucky, we might see one come out. We have to be absolutely quiet—remember platypuses are extremely shy.

There's one! He's diving. He must be hungry. Platypuses use their bills to find food. A platypus bill has tiny organs that sense electrical currents given off by animals—like freshwater shrimp and mollusks—when they move. Cool, huh?

A platypus can stay underwater for as long as 10 minutes, but it will usually surface to breathe after a minute or two.

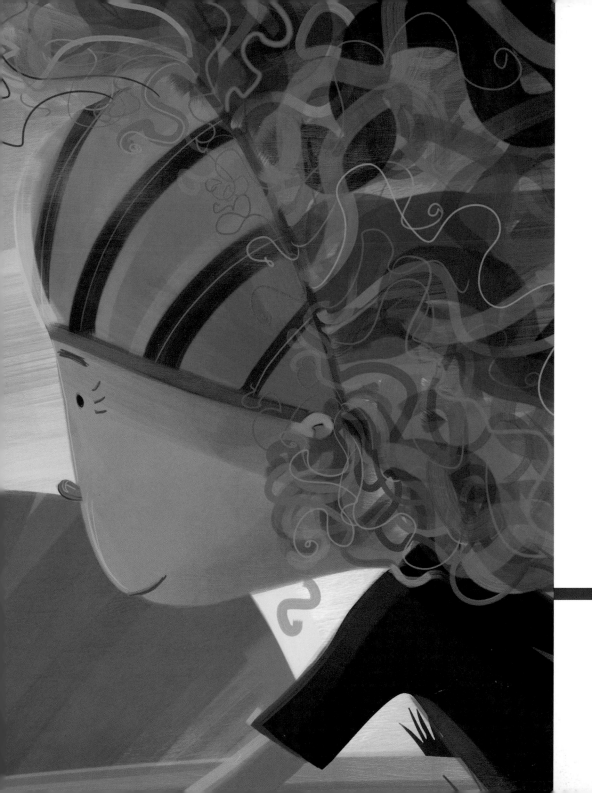

Well, hello!
It's nice to meet
you platypus!

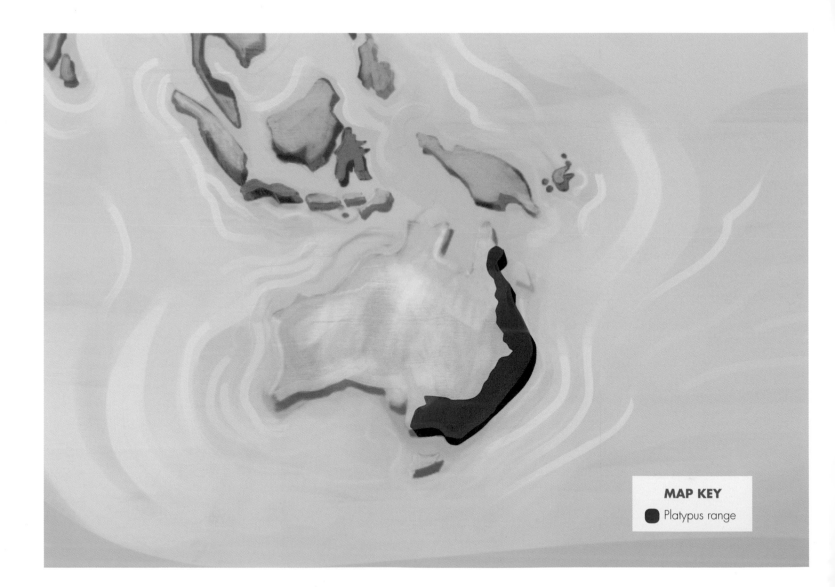

MAP KEY

● Platypus range

GLOSSARY

burrow A hole in the ground made by an animal to use for its home.

mollusk An animal with a soft body and no spine that usually has a shell, such as a snail or clam.

nocturnal Active at night.

venom A poisonous fluid some animals use to defend themselves against other animals.

webbing Skin that is stretched between the toes of an animal that spends a lot of time in or near water; it makes their feet more like paddles.

wombat A burrowing mammal that lives in Australia; it looks like a small bear.

READ MORE

Antill, Sara. **Platypus**. New York: Windmill Books, 2011.

Arnold, Caroline. **A Platypus' World**. Minneapolis: Picture Window Books, 2008.

Berkes, Marianne Collins. Over in Australia: Amazing Animals Down Under. Nevada City, Calif.: Dawn Publishing, 2011.

Murray, Julie. **Platypuses**. Edina, Minn.: ABDO Pub., 2011.

WEBSITES

Duck-billed Platypus Printout—Enchanted Learning.com
http://www.enchantedlearning.com/subjects/mammals/platypus/Duckbillprintout.shtml
Print and color this diagram of a platypus and learn the names of its body parts.

Platypuses—Animal Fact Guide
http://www.animalfactguide.com/animal-facts/platypus/
See pictures and read facts about the platypus.

Platypus Facts and Pictures—National Geographic Kids
http://kids.nationalgeographic.com/kids/animals/creaturefeature/platypus/
Watch a video of a duck-billed platypus waddling around its habitat.

Every effort has been made to ensure that these websites are appropriate for children. However, because of the nature of the Internet, it is impossible to guarantee that these sites will remain active indefinitely or that their contents will not be altered.

Read these exciting books!

978-1-62243-189-2

978-1-62243-190-8

978-1-62243-191-5

978-1-62243-192-2

978-1-62243-193-9

978-1-62243-194-6

978-1-62243-195-3

978-1-62243-196-0

![RiverStream Science logo]
RiverStream Science
Great Reading • Real Learning

Ages 7 and up

DO YOU REALLY WANT TO MEET
A CROCODILE?

DO YOU REALLY WANT TO MEET
A MONKEY?

DO YOU REALLY WANT TO MEET
A PLATYPUS?

DO YOU REALLY WANT TO MEET
A POLAR BEAR?

DO YOU REALLY WANT TO MEET
A SWAN?

DO YOU REALLY WANT TO MEET
A TIGER?

Do You Really Want to Meet Wild Animals?

The animals in the zoo look cute and cuddly...but what if you met them face-to-face in the wild? How do they behave in their own habitats? Imagine yourself as a future biologist as you make firsthand observations of the wild animals that are more dangerous than they look!

819236 01229 5

RiverStream Publishing
P.O. Box 364
Mankato, MN 56002
www.riverstreampublishing.net

ISBN-13: 978-1-62243-229-5

9 781622 432295

Made in the U.S.A.